IMAGES
of America

FORT
MACARTHUR

Lt. Gen. Arthur MacArthur Jr. (1845–1912) is pictured here in 1906. (The MacArthur Memorial, Norfolk, Virginia.)

ON THE COVER: At Don, California, on June 12, 1936, one of Fort MacArthur's 14-inch railway guns fires on a towed target 14 miles off the coast. Simulated wartime conditions were used during this training exercise. Aircraft were used to identify the impact of the shells. (George Ruhlen collection, FMM.)

IMAGES
of America

FORT
MACARTHUR

Stephen R. Nelson and David K. Appel

ARCADIA
PUBLISHING

Published by Arcadia Publishing
Charleston SC, Chicago IL, Portsmouth NH, San Francisco CA

Printed in the United States of America

Library of Congress Catalog Card Number: 2005933804

For all general information contact Arcadia Publishing at:
Telephone 843-853-2070
Fax 843-853-0044
E-mail sales@arcadiapublishing.com
For customer service and orders:
Toll-Free 1-888-313-2665

Visit us on the Internet at www.arcadiapublishing.com

This book is dedicated to
Mr. Pete Demmitt
friend, mentor, volunteer.
He came to Fort MacArthur upon enlisting in 1944
and is still here in 2005!

CONTENTS

INTRODUCTION

At the dawn of the 20th century, the Wild West had been tamed and the United States was organizing the Pacific Coast for increasing trade opportunities. In Los Angeles, continued commercial expansion depended on the development of a sea terminal. The successful establishment of the harbor facilitated rapid commercial expansion, and Los Angeles began to take its place in the national story. A maturing West Coast opened a new frontier and exposed the nation to new peoples, new opportunities, and new potential threats.

In the new century's first decade, real estate speculation in the lands surrounding the harbor caused a frantic dash to develop the shoreline, including the occupation of vacant federal property. Responding to the loss of control of its land, the Department of the Interior transferred holdings to the War Department, providing for government development along with the anticipated commercial growth.

The impetus for military development occurred after the Russo-Japanese War of 1904–1905. With the near completion of the harbor facilities, the War Department recognized that the new harbor might present a target for potential aggressors. The Taft Board recommended that the Los Angeles Harbor be defended from seaborne enemy attack. The War Department envisioned protecting the harbor by fortifying San Pedro. Planners soon determined that existing War Department lands along the shoreline were insufficient for proper defensive positions and a search commenced for additional acreage. In 1910, a large tract of land was purchased for use as the site of several large-caliber gun positions. Located southwest of the existing government land on the bluffs overlooking the harbor, this new area was officially known as the Upper Reservation, called "Topside" by the soldiers. While Topside would serve as the gun emplacements, the administrative and support facilities would be located on the original shoreline land, subdivided into areas termed the Middle and Lower Reservations (later called Middleside and Bottomside, respectively).

Construction of the new fortifications began in 1914, with the gun positions officially completed in 1923. The new fort was named in honor of Lt. Gen. Arthur MacArthur, the Civil War hero and distinguished military leader who foresaw the need to fortify Los Angeles Harbor. Construction and development continued throughout the next 60 years, with the largest increases during World War II and the Cold War.

In 1940, the fort changed from a typical coast defense garrison by assuming the added responsibility of operating one of the nation's largest army induction centers. Fort MacArthur processed 750,000 men for the war effort. In 1946, the fort became a separation center. During the Cold War, it served as the headquarters for the air defenses of the Los Angeles area. The fort's role as defender of Los Angeles began with the big gun era and continued through the Cold War missile era.

In other ways, the fort took the lead in initiating change for both the army and society at large. In the 1920s, the fort offered the Citizens' Military Training Camp (CMTC) program to hundreds of young men. CMTC provided general military indoctrination and specialized training for its participants to create a cadre of trained citizens for the next war. In 1938, Fort MacArthur was chosen as one of the sites for an experimental version of the CMTC program, offering training to African Americans. Of the African American participants, many served in the army during World War II, and a few became accomplished fighter pilots with the famed Tuskegee Airmen. This step towards desegregation of the army contributed to desegregation in society.

Fort MacArthur was arguably the first base to use canine sentries as an integral part of its defensive plans. While some debate exists as to the exact origins of the army's K-9 Corps, Fort MacArthur began experimentation as early as 1940, predating the army's official K-9 Corps start date of 1942. Whatever the outcome of the debate, Fort MacArthur played a key role in the development of canine use by the military.

The fort was also the first and only installation to allow 24-hour access to a non-military private support group. The VACS (Volunteer Army Canteen Service) organization was started by wives of Hollywood film moguls. VACS support of the Fort MacArthur garrison was a tremendous morale booster for the troops and new recruits of the reception center. The VACS special arrangement with the post contributed to women's opportunities and equality during and after war.

In yet another example of Fort MacArthur's ability to improvise, adapt, and lead, the fort's headquarters recognized early on that many of the recruits "caught in the draft" were coming from Hollywood. Often these draftees showed skill and talent that were not ideally suited to regular army life or to the battlefield. Draftees from the entertainment industry were identified from the pool of recruits and placed in special services roles at Fort MacArthur and in greater Los Angeles. Special services activities provided the audiences, who were often separated from family and community for the first time in their lives, a brief escape from the dramatic transition to army life. The ability of Fort MacArthur to use Hollywood talent for morale boosting activities rather than regular military duties shows remarkably proactive personnel management. Some of these Hollywood professionals helped produce *Hey Rookie*, an all-army show that ran for nine months in downtown Los Angeles. The show was such a hit that it was transferred overseas and performed in two different theaters of operation. Overseas the cast earned three campaign stars and the show received a Letter of Commendation from General Eisenhower.

With the beginning of the Cold War in the late 1940s, the War Department began to sense that there would be yet another need for troops. If a war did start, a ready reserve would greatly assist with mobilization. However, World War II had taken a toll on the population's desire to serve. Everyone wanted to return to normal life. Finding men willing to serve in the reserves proved difficult. Taking the lead once again, Fort MacArthur experimented with a program that allowed men to bring their families to their scheduled reserve training. Families were permitted to stay in the vacant quarters built at the height of the war. Soldiers conducted military training by day and spent nights with their families. Bases throughout the country adopted the "Fort MacArthur Plan" as part of their reserve training. Throughout the Cold War, Fort MacArthur continued to be an agent of change. With the deployment of Nike air defense missile system throughout the Los Angeles area, canines returned to the fort. This time, the canines were used to protect the Nikes from sabotage. As the Nike sites were upgraded, Hollywood again joined with the base, this time as part of "Operation Nike," a public relations campaign to increase public support for army air defense activities. In 1966, in one of the fort's proudest Cold War moments, Battery D, 4th Battalion, 251st Air Defense Artillery (California National Guard) scored a 100 percent rating on its Short Notice Annual Practice (SNAP) drill, becoming the first continental army unit (regular or National Guard) to achieve such a score.

In 1974, the Nike program was terminated and Fort MacArthur was slated for closure. Topside was transferred to the City of Los Angeles and split between the Department of Recreation and Parks and the Los Angeles Unified School District. Batteries Osgood-Farley and Barlow-Saxton are listed on the National Register of Historic Places and will be preserved for future generations. Middleside continues a military mission as a support facility for the Los Angeles Air Force Base. Bottomside has had previous fill excavated and serves as a municipal marina for small craft.

The Fort MacArthur Museum operates from Battery Osgood-Farley, housing thousands of artifacts, photographs, and documents. The museum restores and operates a variety of military equipment and vehicles and its staff conducts tours of Topside.

This visual history of Fort MacArthur presents technological, social, and environmental developments that include changes in weapons, changes in structures, and even changes in hairstyles. Different from previous textual histories, this work will show the fort as a mirror of society and illustrate societal change as captured in personal snapshots and professional photographs.

This photographic illustration of the fort's history is limited in breadth and scope but contributes a visual record that has been missing from other works. Photographs appearing here credited as FMM are from the Fort MacArthur Museum Association and are reproduced with the permission of the board of directors. A large portion of the museum's photographs have been obtained directly from the veterans that served at the fort. Photographs used from named collections within the overall museum collection have been identified. These images provide reflections of our society as it progressed through the 20th century.

The authors are donating all royalties directly to the Fort MacArthur Museum Association, a California non-profit corporation established to assist the City of Los Angeles Department of Recreation and Parks with the continued management of the museum. For more information about the museum association, please visit www.ftmac.org.

One

SAN PEDRO WILL
BE FORTIFIED!

"San Pedro Will Be Fortified" is the headline from a 1910 San Pedro newspaper. When Congress approved the construction of a fort overlooking Los Angeles Harbor, responsibility was given to the U.S. Army Corps of Engineers. Los Angeles was a relative latecomer to coastal fortifications, but the corps was ready for the undertaking having gained experience from the earlier Taft-era construction program. The following images come from the construction period during 1916–1919, and most come from the Corps of Engineers (CE) photographic record of the construction. The first troops to garrison Fort MacArthur were members of 4th Company Coast Artillery Corps from Fort Scott. They arrived on March 23, 1917, and their new title became 1st Company Fort MacArthur. They had a short stay before global events took them overseas.

U.S. Engineer Department trucks prepare for work on the Fort MacArthur Upper Reservation around 1915. (CE-LA District collection, FMM.)

Loading bays, seen at Fort MacArthur on September 14, 1915, filled aggregate trucks that hauled materials to concrete plants built at various batteries under construction. (CE-LA District collection, FMM.)

Excavation and form installation are seen at 12-inch seacoast mortar Batteries Saxton and John Barlow. (CE-LA District collection, FMM.)

On October 23, 1915, the right flank of the mortar batteries shows excavation for shot gallery and magazine of right flank pit. (CE-LA District collection, FMM.)

Room forms, before lagging (vertical support pieces applied to the frame) and skin (wood sheathing) are applied, are seen on September 1, 1915, at the left flank of 12-inch seacoast mortar Batteries Saxton and John Barlow. (CE-LA District collection, FMM.)

In November 1915, form construction is visible at the right flank of mortar Batteries Saxton and John Barlow. (CE-LA District collection, FMM.)

An overview of the construction of rifle battery site A (Osgood-Farley) on December 16, 1916, shows various technologies used during construction, including the steam-powered crane (right), internal combustion engine on the truck (center), and horse-drawn wagon (left). The large tower in the center is part of the concrete mixing plant. Concrete was pumped to the top, then directed, by a flume, to the various forms. (CE-LA District collection, FMM.)

Capt. A. H. Archer, CE, pictured on June 9, 1917, was the construction officer for Fort MacArthur. (CE-LA District collection, FMM.)

Concrete tiles to protect the waterproofing treatment of the batteries were produced in a special plant built specifically to manufacture the tiles. (CE-LA District collection, FMM: November 23, 1915.)

Battery Osgood-Farley had concrete tiles lying over the waterproofing treatment to protect it. (CE-LA District collection, FMM: October 23, 1915.)

Armored electrical lines and heavy-duty light fixtures were installed at the entrance of the power plant in Batteries Barlow and John Saxton. (CE-LA District collection, FMM: June 9, 1919.)

Two General Electric 25-kilowatt generators were inside Battery Leary-Merriam, c. 1919. The coast artillery was the first branch of the army to utilize electricity on a major scale and the first to employ electricians as part of the trained cadre. (CE-LA District collection, FMM.)

A disappearing carriage was installed at site B (Leary-Merriam) for a 14-inch gun. (CE-LA District collection, FMM: December 15, 1916.)

This 14-inch gun was added into the Osgood pit of Battery Osgood-Farley in 1923, but the process illustrated is similar to that used with all of the 14-inch gun installation at Fort MacArthur. The battery commander's station is on the hill in the upper right. Originally these stations were exposed to the elements, but they were later enclosed to protect the delicate optical instruments inside. (George Ruhlen collection, FMM.)

The installation of the enormous 14-inch gun at the Osgood gun pit in 1923 required the use of heavy timbers and rolling gear. (George Ruhlen collection, FMM.)

In 1917, this 14-inch disappearing gun was newly installed in the Farley gun pit of Battery Osgood-Farley. (FMM.)

A 12-inch seacoast mortar barrel is being hauled to Batteries Saxton and John Barlow in 1916. The Corps of Engineers used the Allen Brothers Trucking Company to haul the heavy equipment from the Middle Reservation to the batteries. Legend has it that the weight of the equipment burned up the engines in several trucks, after which horses and mules were used to haul the equipment up the steep hills. (CE-LA District collection, FMM.)

Installation of the 12-inch seacoast mortar barrels into their carriages occurred in December 1916, as construction workers continued work on the motor pit and battery. (CE-LA District collection, FMM.)

On January 27, 1917, battery and pit work is complete and brand-new, 12-inch seacoast mortars await soldiers. (CE-LA District collection, FMM.)

After the guns and mortars were installed, Fort MacArthur began receiving new equipment such as this state-of-the-art searchlight and Cadillac truck that served as both the light's prime mover and power generator. Records indicate that there were at least six of these mobile searchlight units assigned to the fort. Lights were loaded onto the back end of the trucks for transportation. (CE-LA District collection, FMM: September 15, 1921.)

While the batteries were being constructed Topside, the Quartermaster Corps was busy building new gun crew barracks Middleside. The recently completed barracks on the northwest side of Patton Quadrangle don't yet have completed landscaping, c. 1918. (FMM.)

Officers also needed a place to stay. Newly completed by the Quartermaster Corps, these garrison officers' quarters are ready to occupy, with the commanding officer's house center left just behind the sign, c. 1918. The sign illustrates some security concerns of the time and also has a curious spelling of Point "Firmin." Point Fermin is about one mile south. (FMM.)

Two

WORLD WAR I

World War I brought new challenges to the fort. The war was fought primarily in Europe, and Fort MacArthur, with its fixed armament facing the Pacific, was geographically removed from the fighting. There was little possibility of the Fort MacArthur soldiers joining the fight in the role for which they had trained. The 1st Company was redesignated as the 3rd Anti-Aircraft (AA) Battery and shipped out on November 30, 1917. In early 1918, many of the fort's troops were organized into ammunition train detachments for service overseas. The 52nd and 53rd Ammunition Trains were largely made up of Fort MacArthur soldiers. Other units receiving Fort MacArthur troops included the 2nd Anti-Aircraft Battalion, the 2nd Army Artillery, the 55th Ammunition Train, and the 19th Regiment of Artillery. While mustering of various units heading overseas brought significant changes, certain aspects of garrison life—the company mess halls, troop formations, and barracks life—remained familiar. Images from the World War I cantonment areas depict the daily activities of soldiers about to go to war, while other scenes reflect the sparse nature of the newly finished structures throughout the fort.

These troops are believed to have been selected for ammunition train or anti-aircraft duty in France. They are seen at the Upper Reservation cantonment in 1918. The structures in the right background are thought to be NCO housing that was torn down in the late 1930s or early 1940s. (FMM.)

The troops in formation outside this barracks in the cantonment are equipped with M1917 Enfield rifles. (FMM: 1918.)

The buildings in the Topside cantonment were little more than wooden slats and tarpaper roofs and were, according to some veterans, very hot. This is the central road of the cantonment around 1918. (FMM.)

Soldiers ate in mess halls that were constructed like the barracks. This wooden sidewalk bridges the drainage ditch. The hillside consists of a thick, clay soil that, when wet, adhered to any form of footwear. (FMM.)

This mess hall is complete with Post Toasties cereal and an ample supply of beans! These soldiers use their field mess gear, while the permanent garrison used china and flatware. These troops were in either a transient status or a training cycle around 1918. (FMM.)

The interior of the YMCA exhibits the permanent construction characteristics found on Middleside and is likely to have been located there. (FMM: 1918.)

While the troops were training for overseas duty, the main armament of the fort was placed in caretaker mode. Here is the pristine 14-inch disappearing gun from the Leary pit of Battery Leary-Merriam, complete with two-tone paint job and breech cover, c. 1918. (FMM.)

Middleside was busy with the influx of soldiers being mustered for duty on the ammunition trains or anti-aircraft units. The post guardhouse on the south side of the quadrangle (with the photographer's humorous caption) attested to the inevitability of interpersonal conflicts. The saluting gun in the foreground was replaced by French 75-mm field guns after World War I. (FMM: 1918.)

The Fort Mac Arthur Convalescence Ward on Pacific Avenue was probably built for soldiers recuperating from injuries received overseas. There was a more permanent hospital building nearby. (FMM: 1918.)

Around 1918, the permanent hospital structure was built in the same style as the other Middleside buildings. (FMM.)

Three

BETWEEN THE WARS

The interwar period at the fort, 1919–1940, were years of dramatic change. From the demobilization after the Great War through the Great Depression, new technologies and units arrived and departed from the fort. In the 1920s, the National Guard used the fort extensively. Shortly after the Great War, three companies of coast artillery troops were assigned to the fort, and in 1922, those companies became Headquarters Battery and Batteries A and B, 3rd Coast Artillery. In 1924, the army reconstituted the 3rd Coast Artillery Regiment, which became the first coast artillery regiment to garrison the post. Later that year, the Los Angeles Harbor Defense fortifications were reduced to only skeletal manning when the regiment sent battalions to garrison Fort Rosecrans, overlooking San Diego Bay and Fort Stevens at the mouth of the Columbia River. The regiment's main armament was augmented in 1927 by the first of two enormous 14-inch railway guns. These guns gave the regiment and the community a new attraction. In 1929, the severely reduced strength of the 3rd Coast Artillery was augmented by the arrival of the 63rd Coast Artillery (Anti-Aircraft) from Fort Scott in San Francisco. This unit dominated the fort throughout the 1930s. They brought the latest weapons and equipment for anti-aircraft defense to the Los Angeles Harbor. In the late 1920s and throughout the 1930s, Fort MacArthur had the additional mission of hosting the Citizens' Military Training Camp (CMTC) program that brought young men into the world of the army for one month each summer. Stellar graduates of the complete four-summer program could apply for reserve commissions. The 63rd Coast Artillery hosted the CMTC program and often used coast artillery reserve officers. This provided the reservists and the recruits with their annual training in a single combined training cycle. The CMTC program at Fort MacArthur was later expanded to include a segregated cycle for African Americans. This unique opportunity for young black citizens was part of a national project spurred on by Eleanor Roosevelt and African American leaders. In the late 1930s, National Guard, CMTC, and reserve training slowly faded into obscurity as the world plunged into another war.

On July 1, 1924, the 3rd Artillery was reconstituted as the 3rd Coast Artillery Regiment on the Fort MacArthur parade ground. Officers' houses are seen in the background. (George Ruhlen collection, FMM.)

Brig. Gen. William Kobbe and Maj. George Ruhlen address the formation at the reconstitution ceremony. Brigadier General Kobbe commanded elements of the 3rd Artillery in the Philippines. Major Ruhlen was the first commanding officer of the reconstituted 3rd Coast Artillery Regiment and had an extensive career in the coast artillery. (George Ruhlen collection, FMM.)

Guidons of the 3rd Coast Artillery assemble at the reconstitution ceremony. Headquarters Battery and Batteries A and B were stationed at Fort MacArthur, while the 2nd Battalion with Battery D was sent to Fort Rosecrans and 3rd Battalion with Battery E was sent to Fort Stevens, Oregon. (George Ruhlen collection, FMM.)

New regimental colors of the 3rd Coast Artillery were presented at the reconstitution ceremony. (George Ruhlen collection, FMM.)

The 3rd Artillery (predecessor of 3rd Coast Artillery) regimental colors, detailing the battles of the regiment dating from the War of 1812, was displayed at the reconstitution ceremony. This flag was mounted, framed, and hung in the commander's office until the end of World War II. Its whereabouts are currently unknown. (George Ruhlen collection, FMM.)

The 251st Coast Artillery Regiment (Harbor Defense) of the California National Guard (CNG) was established in 1924 from elements including the 468th Company, Coast Artillery Corps (CNG). The 251st Regiment, and other CNG units, frequently conducted summer field training on the Upper Reservation. The CNG continued to play a significant role at Fort MacArthur for decades to follow. (R. W. Gastil collection, FMM: August 1924.)

Members of the 251st Coast Artillery (Harbor Defense) color guard, attired in First World War–style service uniform with visor caps and flag carriers, participate in the first summer training opening ceremonies. (R. W. Gastil collection, FMM.)

During summer field training in August 1924, members of the 251st Coast Artillery trained on the Merriam 14-inch gun of Battery Leary-Merriam. Gun crews wore denim (fatigue) uniforms, while wool uniforms were worn by range and plotting crews. (R. W. Gastil collection, FMM.)

Members of the 251st Coast Artillery also trained with the 12-inch seacoast mortars of Batteries Saxton and John Barlow. There were eight mortars in this battery. (R. W. Gastil collection, FMM: August 1925.)

In August 1925, shot carts and shells are ready for the 251st Coast Artillery practice firing at the Osgood 14-inch gun of Battery Osgood-Farley. (R. W. Gastil collection, FMM.)

In August 1925, members of the 251st Coast Artillery prepare to load the 14-inch Osgood gun of Battery Osgood-Farley. (R. W. Gastil collection, FMM.)

The 1,460 pound, 14-inch shells were moved from the magazine area into the gun pits on shot carts, *c.* 1925. At the entrance to the Osgood gun pit, soldiers are wearing the blue denim fatigue uniform used by gun crews. This uniform was also made in khaki denim, and both types were worn by all members of the army for fatigue duty. (FMM.)

In this August 1924 photograph, 251st Coast Artillery men pause in gun drill after loading the Farley gun. Soldiers are holding the rammer and have moved away the empty shot cart. (R. W. Gastil collection, FMM.)

One can almost feel the anticipation of these young 251st Coast Artillery guardsmen waiting for the firing of the guns shown in a very rare interior photograph in August 1925 of the Osgood-Farley battery commander's (BC) station. The BC station is equipped with a M1910 Azimuth instrument and EE-70 telephone sets. (R. W. Gastil collection, FMM.)

In August 1924, gun crewmen have moved away and the Osgood 14-inch gun is ready! (R. W. Gastil collection, FMM.)

At a "fire" command in August 1924, the destructive power of a 14-inch shell is hurled toward a towed target 10 miles at sea. Most gun crewmen have moved to the very edges of the pit. The photograph has apparently been censored as evidenced by the scratches in the image above the gun. (R. W. Gastil collection, FMM.)

Although immensely popular with the troops, the firing practices were not appreciated by the civilian community—especially as the area became more populated. (R. W. Gastil collection, FMM: August 1924.)

In August 1925, guardsmen load a 12-inch mortar in Batteries Saxton and John Barlow. The leather pouch carried by the man near the breech contains the primers for igniting the propelling charge. The teamwork necessary in loading and firing mortars is as critical as with the disappearing rifles of the other batteries. (R. W. Gastil collection, FMM.)

Crewmembers now recount that firing these mortars was a brutal experience. Since the muzzle was lower than the battery structure, the concussion was confined. Some men recall having their clothing torn and their eardrums ruptured by the blasts. (R. W. Gastil collection, FMM: August 1925.)

A coast artillery round impacts close offshore in 1924. The inscription on the reverse of this photograph reads, "Test firing the Osgood gun." Note the dust coming off the ground from the blast. (George Ruhlen collection, FMM.)

In August 1925, observers for the firing were placed in various fixed positions around the hillside and equipped with a BC telescope model 1910 and a EE 70 telephone set. The campaign hat and wrap leggings (puttees) were typical uniforms for troops not working directly on the guns or with the ammunition. (R. W. Gastil collection, FMM.)

At the end of every firing, the guns were thoroughly cleaned. At the end of each training cycle, the guns were covered with a heavy coat of cosmoline to protect and preserve it for the next use. Sometimes the intervals between firing lasted more than a year. (FMM: 1920s.)

Duty at the fort was not restricted to firing practice and drills but could involve public relations activities, as evidenced by members of Battery E, 251st Coast Artillery (Harbor Defense, CNG) marching in the 1927 San Pedro Armistice Day Parade. Battery E was stationed in San Pedro, while the other batteries were in Long Beach and San Diego. (San Pedro VFW collection, FMM.)

National Guard soldiers were not the only ones assigned to the November 1927 parade. The 3rd Coast Artillery Regiment Band also participated. Facing the camera is band member Stanley Clark, who served in both the Mexican Punitive Expedition and with the Siberian Expeditionary Force at the end of World War I. He served several tours at the fort before retiring after nearly 30 years of army service. (San Pedro VFW collection, FMM.)

Parade service involved unique opportunities to demonstrate the patriotism of the Armed Forces. Here participants commemorate Armistice Day in November 1927. (San Pedro VFW collection, FMM.)

In November 1927, soldiers were assigned to ride the floats of a number of local civic groups, including one from the local Ku Klux Klan. Fear-based isolationist groups expanded dramatically in the late 1920s. Shortly after World War I, Ku Klux Klan membership rose as it expressed an isolationist attitude in addition to participating in racist activities. Fear accompanied the United States as it headed toward the Great Depression. (San Pedro VFW collection, FMM.)

In February 1926, the fort's armament was upgraded to include the first of two 14-inch railway guns, which were the army's largest mobile guns. The gun was put on display for the public at the Middle Reservation on its semi-permanent mount. The fort used this tower for its radio communications system. (FMM.)

Because firing railway guns from the Middle Reservation could cause severe damage to nearby structures and houses, the guns were transported to prearranged firing positions at Don, near Oceanside, and at Naples, near Goleta. Here, on June 11, 1936, the guns are on their way to the Don firing site. (FMM.)

The army moved the railway guns into firing positions, the same way they could be relocated in the event of war. On June 11, 1936, 3rd Coast Artillery soldiers are pretending to fire .30-caliber machine guns at enemy planes during the railroad movement. (FMM.)

On June 12, 1936, the railway gun is nearly ready for firing. Once in position, the guns required much preparation, including setting outriggers and supports. Although designed to fire from the tracks, eyewitnesses say it actually damaged them. (George Ruhlen collection, FMM.)

A round is fired on June 12, 1936. Firing the guns always drew crowds of spectators and VIPs. (George Ruhlen collection, FMM.)

This time the gun is viewed from the opposite side. The cans on the right contained powder bags. The tents on the left were set up for gun crews. This photograph's caption says that the guns are firing "at a moving target 23 miles at sea" and that "it was the first time they had been fired in eight years." (Associated Press photograph, FMM: June 12, 1936.)

Both railway guns fired almost simultaneously. On June 12, 1936, the support cars (boxcars) that formed part of the train accompany each gun into firing position. (George Ruhlen collection, FMM.)

The railway gun appears on the Middle Reservation semi-permanent mount around 1930. Armor-piercing shells (ready ammunition) are at hand because of the time required to move the shells from the magazines. In case of seaward attack, the ready ammunition would be fired while other troops were hauling fresh rounds from the magazine. (Ralph Featherolf collection, FMM.)

In 1929, the 63rd Coast Artillery (Anti-Aircraft) was sent to Fort MacArthur from Fort Winfield Scott in San Francisco. The three-inch anti-aircraft gun (equipped with mascot) is on the Upper Reservation firing range in 1931. (Capt. W. P. Robinson collection, FMM.)

One of the 63rd Coast Artillery's most important tasks, other than providing anti-aircraft protection for the fort, was to administer annual training for Army Reserve officers. In August 1934, the 519th Coast Artillery (AA, Reserve) is setting up three-inch guns on the Upper Reservation in preparation for their annual drill. The guns and enlisted soldiers needed in the drill came from the 63rd Coast Artillery (AA) since the 519th had no enlisted men or equipment of its own. (Charles H. Scott collection, FMM.)

The 63rd had some of the most advanced anti-aircraft equipment in the U.S. Army inventory. In 1939, Capt. Charles H. Scott, 519th Coast Artillery, gives instruction on the height finder. This instrument used stereoscopic range findings to provide more accurate readings than coincidence range finding. (Charles H. Scott collection, FMM.)

The gun director computed information from the height finder and transmitted that information to the gun crews for setting the fuses on their shells. In 1934, members of the 519th Coast Artillery (Reserve) set up an M1 Director in preparation for their annual drill. (Charles H. Scott collection, FMM.)

Three-inch anti-aircraft guns fire at the Upper Reservation firing range. These are 63rd Coast Artillery (AA) guns and crews supervised by reserve officers from the 519th during their 1939 annual drill. (Charles H. Scott collection, FMM.)

Sound locators were important tools used to direct searchlights to airborne targets during night operations. At the annual drill in 1939, the M1A1 Sound Locator is positioned at the Upper Reservation in preparation for a 519th night-firing exercise. (Charles H. Scott collection, FMM.)

Complete night-fighting equipment for the three-inch guns included M1939 searchlights, M1939 searchlight Distant Electrical Control units (DECs), and M1A1 Sound Locators. Members of the 63rd Coast Artillery (AA) pose with night-fighting equipment in preparation for the 519th's training. The DEC, located in the center of the photograph, normally was positioned 150–200 feet away from the light. Sound locators picked up the target, transmitted information to the light crews, and DECs and lights would find the target and track it until it was destroyed by the guns or moved out of range. (Charles H. Scott collection, FMM: 1939.)

Sound locators used fairly simple technology—large horns connected to amplifiers and headsets. The crew simply pointed the horns towards the sound. Other controllers read the azimuth and elevations from the locator and communicated with the searchlight crews. (Charles H. Scott collection, FMM: 1939.)

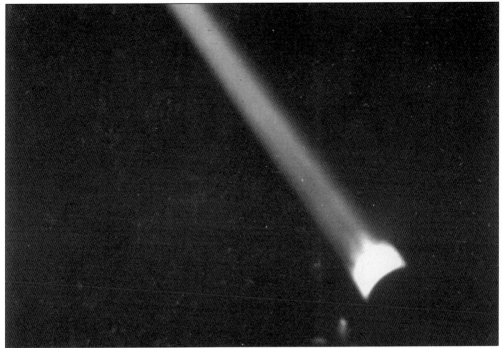

An anti-aircraft searchlight of the 63rd Coast Artillery turns its beam skyward during the 519th Coast Artillery annual practice in 1939. (Charles H. Scott collection, FMM.)

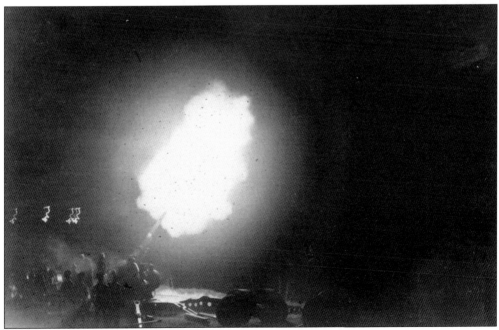

In 1939, a three-inch, anti-aircraft gun fires during night practice at the Upper Reservation range. (Charles H. Scott collection, FMM.)

The three-inch gun was the main armament for high-altitude attack, but machine guns were essential for low-level attacks. The 63rd Coast Artillery (AA) M1917A1 .30-caliber, water-cooled Brownings open fire from the special M1 (AA) mount in 1939. (Charles H. Scott collection, FMM.)

Machine gun crews fired at target "sleeves" towed behind aircraft flying over the Catalina Channel. In 1934, the crew is firing a .30-caliber machine gun at a target sleeve that is outside the frame of the photograph. (Charles H. Scott collection, FMM.)

The results of the machine gun firing on the target sleeve are examined following range fire. The photograph inscription reads, "There are many holes in the sleeve!" (Charles H. Scott collection, FMM.)

The M2 Browning .50-caliber water-cooled machine gun was another anti-aircraft weapon. It is on the same M1 (AA) mount used with the .30-caliber machine guns and is equipped with a "tombstone" magazine and a unique flash hider attached to the muzzle (perhaps to prevent night blindness of the gunner). Ammunition was more expensive for the .50-caliber guns, thus the .30-calibers were used far more frequently. The crewman in the foreground is seated on the water circulation pump for the gun. (Charles H. Scott collection, FMM: 1939.)

In 1934, members of the 519th Coast Artillery parade on the Middle Reservation. Two 14-inch railway guns are elevated in the background. (Charles H. Scott collection, FMM.)

In August 1939, Citizens' Military Training Camp (CMTC) cadets arrive at the Upper Reservation. The 63rd Coast Artillery and 519th Coast Artillery (Reserve) supervised the annual CMTC camps. CMTC was designed to give four annual practice sessions to young men in their teens and twenties to establish a ready reserve of soldiers in case of war. Fort MacArthur conducted these camps from the late 1920s to 1940. (Charles H. Scott collection, FMM.)

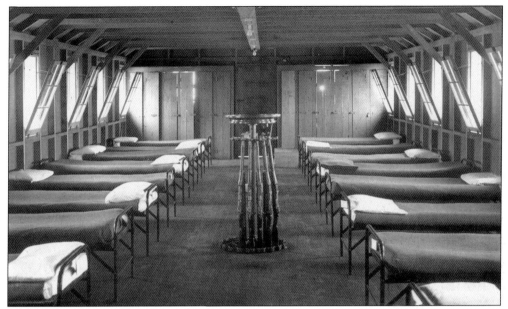

This was home for one month each summer for the CMTC cadets. The training cycle was intended to run for four consecutive summers. The first course was called the Basics, followed by Red, White, and Blue courses. At the end of the cycle, cadets could apply for a reserve commission. This circular rifle rack contains M1903 Springfield rifles. (Clarence Burns collection, FMM.)

CMTC cadets were given all of the basic tasks of regular soldiers. In 1931, this group of cadets learns the fine art of spud peeling outside the World War I Upper Reservation barracks. (FMM.)

Physical training, such as this race, was also a key part of the CMTC experience. Special medals and trophies were given to the winning cadets, c. 1930. (FMM.)

In 1931, CMTC students are instructed on the three-inch M1918 mobile AA gun. The cadets were issued World War I–era uniforms, with puttees for leggings and special CMTC collar insignia. The three-inch M1903 rapid-fire seacoast guns in the background were once part of Battery Lodor on Deadman's Island. They were stored at the Upper Reservation after their removal. (FMM.)

Here CMTC cadets fire three-inch M1918 AA guns. Many former cadets recall fondly their experiences, especially being well fed and getting to fire many different types of weapons. (FMM: 1931.)

After much prodding from Eleanor Roosevelt, the army, in 1938, opened CMTC training to black youth. The segregated program was presented in only a few locations in the country. Fort MacArthur had the special distinction of being one of those selected. In 1939, this chow hall on the Upper Reservation was used by black cadets. (Robert Taylor collection, FMM: 1939.)

African American CMTC cadets fire .30-caliber machine guns on the Upper Reservation. A number of these cadets recall their CMTC experience as one of the best in their lives. Black soldiers from Fort Huachuca, Arizona, were brought in to assist with the training. Many of the CMTC cadets joined the army during World War II, some serving with distinction as Tuskegee Airmen. (Robert Taylor collection, FMM.)

Dances were among the most popular events for cadets. Some dances were local, while others were held as far away as Ventura. Formal military decorum was required, helping to improve the cadets' social skills in addition to their military training. One of the last weekly CMTC dances was held at the fort in 1940. CMTC 1941 was cancelled, as war clouds loomed over Fort MacArthur. (FMM.)

Four

THE BUILDUP FOR WAR

Many political and military leaders believed that the United States would be drawn into the wars raging in Europe and Asia. However, many citizens retreated into isolationist mode, neither wanting nor expecting actual U.S. involvement. In proposing a peacetime draft, President Roosevelt and the military were attempting to establish a pool of trained U.S. citizens that could be mobilized if hostilities arose. Even considering the isolationist sentiment in the country, the draft's promise of a year and a day of service did not seem excessive to many. The U.S. Army grew tremendously with the passage of the 1940 Selective Service Act. Fort MacArthur, the main U.S. Army post in Southern California, had an induction facility on its Lower Reservation. The fort was soon selected as a regional induction facility for new recruits. In addition to the new induction center, the 63rd Coast Artillery (AA) was ordered to Fort Bliss and the remote battalions of the 3rd Coast Artillery ordered permanently reassigned to units at Fort Rosecrans, California, and Fort Stevens, Oregon. Thus, Fort MacArthur was required to rebuild the 3rd Coast Artillery with new recruits. Many came from Indiana and West Virginia, but soon they were all coast artillerymen, ready to defend Los Angeles. While the military prepared for war, the civilian sector still thought in peacetime terms. Labor disputes and strikes were common and even came to Los Angeles. The men of the fort were caught between feeling sympathy for the work force, which they would reenter at the end of their military service, and fulfilling their strike-busting duty as soldiers. Despite the turmoil in the labor force, most of the country sought to return to stability ending a slow climb from the depths of the Depression. At the close of 1941, both soldiers and civilians knew their lives would change, but not in the way they expected. The photographs in this chapter reflect the reconstruction of the 3rd Coast Artillery and some of the experiences of young men "caught in the draft."

These selectees have just arrived at the Fort MacArthur Reception Center and are receiving their first instruction. Arriving at noon, the men were given a brief introduction by a non-commissioned officer, who then escorted them to the barracks for bunk assignment. The group was then lead en masse to the cafeteria-style mess hall. After lunch, the recruits underwent an afternoon of interviews and testing. Once the recruit had been examined and tested, he was assigned an occupational specification and awaited further clothing issue and training. (FMM.)

The Quartermaster Depot at Fort MacArthur issued clothing and equipment to the new men. Regardless of future assignments, soldiers were all issued the same basic kit at the induction center. Later their basic issue may be augmented by specialized equipment required for their specific occupations. (FMM.)

"They came in all shapes and sizes," recalls Gloria (Picazo) Rubio, who served as processing secretary for the new selectees. This is the shoe (or boot) section of the Quartermaster Depot. Rubio saved this c. 1941 photograph because it clearly showed the wide size range of the recruits. (Gloria [Picazo] Rubio collection, FMM.)

These recruits have just received their uniforms and equipment and are now ready for formal training and service. (FMM: 1941.)

Some of the first selectees to arrive at Fort MacArthur had been inducted elsewhere and already had uniforms; however, some were obsolete World War I styles. Pvts. Earl J. Mohlke and William Krause received new uniforms when they were inducted at Fort Harrison, Indiana, in January 1941. Mohlke recalls that most men were issued old uniforms. Krause was issued breeches instead of straight-legged trousers. Veterans have related that shortly after their arrival at Fort MacArthur, they participated in a Middleside parade. When commanding officer Col. Allen Kimberly witnessed the odd arrangement of uniforms, he ordered the whole group back to the reception center for proper ones. (Earl J. Mohlke collection, FMM.)

In 1941, recruits perform calisthenics at the reception center. Physical conditioning was one of the first objectives of military training. (Earl J. Mohlke collection, FMM.)

New soldiers are being taught the basics of the M1903 Springfield rifle. The first batch of recruits was assigned directly to Fort MacArthur and the Harbor Defenses of Los Angeles (HDLA). These troops, mostly from Indiana and West Virginia, were chosen to rebuild the 3rd Coast Artillery that had been split between three Pacific Coast forts in the 1930s. Rebuilding the regiment required nearly 1,500 men. (FMM: 1941.)

In 1941, Lt. Arthur J. Hochuli instructs members of D Battery, 3rd Coast Artillery on the Azimuth instrument—M1910A1. The soldier in the left foreground is Alexander Esparza. These soldiers have new one-piece herringbone twill coveralls designed to replace the old two-piece blue denim fatigues. Both were worn during the early stages of World War II. (FMM.)

Men of the battery rotated through one of the most well-known military duties—the spud-peeling task of the kitchen police (KP). Soldiers that showed an aptitude and interest in this duty were retained or encouraged to stay, as food was critical for morale and mess sergeants sought out the best. Troops selected for KP duty based on punishment normally were not given food-handling tasks, instead they were usually assigned clean-up duties. (FMM: 1941.)

In 1941, this mess hall kitchen is in operation at the Middleside barracks. Art Earick, third from left, was selected for kitchen duty and is preparing food for the men of Battery C under the watchful eye of S.Sgt. Jarrell Newberry. Newberry was a gifted manager, recognized as one of the fort's finest mess sergeants. (FMM.)

In 1941, a mess sergeant was allotted a small amount of cash for each soldier in the battery. The sergeant would then arrange menus and purchase food from local vendors. A crooked mess sergeant could make money for himself by selecting food of inferior quality. Punishment for such offences was severe, and because soldiers would not stand for inferior food, the crooks were often discovered quickly. Dining for the coast artillery was family style—12 men per table with vitreous china—not the cafeteria-style dining of the reception center. (FMM.)

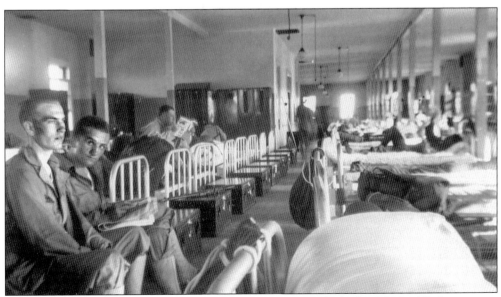

Battery C troops prepare for field exercises with leggings, packs, and rifles. The Middle Reservation barracks, built in 1918, seem rather nice and spacious in 1941. (Floyd D. Lee collection, FMM.)

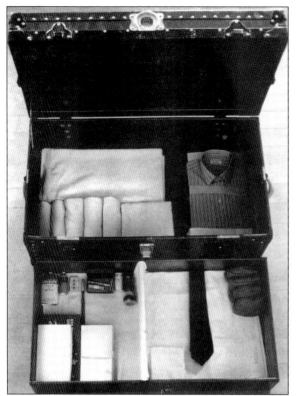

This footlocker, belonging to Guy R. (Dick) Shields of Battery D, 3rd Coast Artillery, is typical of those at the fort in the 1940s. Civilian clothes were common in the prewar years. (Dick Shields collection, FMM: 1941.)

In 1941, Shield's wall locker displays typical arrangement, including the M1917A1 helmet and field gear on top. (Dick Shields collection, FMM.)

With basic training complete, new soldiers were trained on the main armament of the fort. In 1941, these mobile 155-mm GPF guns were used by the Examination Battery, Topside, as well as with the various remote batteries along the coast. (Jack Butts collection, FMM.)

F Battery drills on the 12-inch seacoast mortars at Battery Barlow-Saxton. In 1941, these troops are using the same equipment that was installed during the First World War. This should provide an idea of the severely restricted budget of the army during the 1920s and 1930s. (FMM.)

The disappearing rifles of Battery Leary-Merriam had been in caretaker status for nearly a decade by the time Battery C manned them again in 1941. During a training exercise in mid-1941, the newly trained recruits scored a direct hit on their target and were awarded the prestigious "E" patch, worn on the right cuff of their service uniforms to designate battery excellence in firing excercises. (FMM.)

When the 63rd Coast Artillery (AA) left the fort in December 1940, the anti-aircraft mission was assigned as an additional responsibility to the mortar men of Battery F, 3rd Coast Artillery. Three-inch AA guns are set up along the road leading from Paseo del Mar to Battery Osgood-Farley, c. 1941. (FMM.)

Battery A was assigned to the 14-inch railway guns at the Lower Reservation. One of the guns was on open display for the public in 1941, before the war began. The smaller sub-caliber gun mounted to the top of the barrel was used in training, as the ammunition was far cheaper. Drill round and dummy powder bags needed for crew drill are seen on the cranes. The drill round had a large spring inside attached to a plunger on its base. The plunger compressed the spring when the shell was seated in the breech. When pressure was removed, the plunger kicked back and unseated the round for the next drill. (Union Pacific collection, Los Angles Public Library.)

Firing the fixed seacoast guns involved the use of remote fire control positions called base end stations (BES). BES were surveyed and placed on a known line forming the base of a triangle that allowed for precision fire control. This station for the 12-inch seacoast mortars of Battery Barlow-Saxton was located at Sea Bench, on the coast northwest from the Upper Reservation. Two instruments are inside—an Azimuth instrument and a Depression Position Finder (DPF). The DPF could determine the target's range without using another base end station. (Jack Butts collection, FMM.)

This is the interior of the Sea Bench BES of Battery Barlow-Saxton illustrating good details of the M1 DPF. There were numerous positions like this throughout the hillsides of the Palos Verdes peninsula. In mid-1941, the soldier in this photograph, Jack Butts, was assigned to this station about four days per week. (Jack Butts collection, FMM.)

"When they are eight miles out to sea, the targets used for the practice of firing the large caliber weapons cannot be seen with the naked eye," recalled Battery F veteran Jack Butts. They can only be viewed with the optics in the BC station or a BES. (Jack Butts collection, FMM: c. 1941.)

The practice firing of the 14-inch railway guns on August 15, 1941, created a well-remembered incident when the tremendous concussion from the first shot completely destroyed the makeshift barracks of Battery A, which had been converted from a motor pool shed. As the building collapsed, veterans recall seeing a cloud of underwear on either side of the structure. (Earl J. Mohlke collection, FMM.)

Witnesses recount that every window in San Pedro, from Twenty-second Street back to Sixth Street, was broken when the guns went off. The commanding officer, Col. W. W. Hicks was presented with a $50,000 glass bill from the community. It marked the last time that either of the guns was fired. (Earl J. Mohlke collection, FMM.)

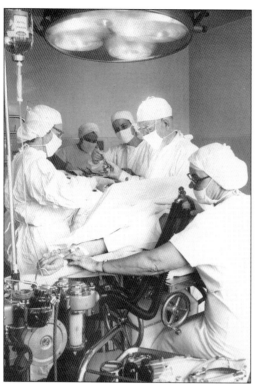

The medical staff is shown in 1941 operating at the Fort MacArthur hospital. Maintaining a soldier's health was a critical job, and with the influx of thousands of new recruits, the hospital was kept busy. Most operations were appendectomies or other common procedures. (Wayne "Dusty" Harris collection, FMM.)

Some medical procedures were intrusive but in other ways. Venereal disease was a serious threat to the fighting soldier, and as such, contraction of the disease was a court martial offense usually resulting in a reduction in rank and assignment to unpleasant tasks. In severe cases, soldiers were kicked out of the army. In 1941, men of Battery E, 3rd Coast Artillery prepare for a periodic "short arm" examination. Raincoats and boots were the uniform of the hour. (Robert Rose collection, FMM.)

The Medical Corps officers at Fort MacArthur assembled a first rate band for their club. As recruits came through the reception center, all had medical exams, at which time the officers also searched for talent. Pvts. Roy Blalock and Royce Woolery were selected for Medical Corps duty as musicians rather than for any medical experience. (Wayne "Dusty" Harris collection, FMM: *c.* 1941.)

The hospital officers called their band MEDICOS, renowned as the finest dance orchestra in the area. In 1941, Dusty Harris (seated fourth from right) entered the army to be a gunner on a B-17, but when the medical officers at the reception center noted his work experience—he had played for Lena Horne, Les Barnett, and other leading bands of the time—they quickly diverted his path from the Air Corps to the Medical Corps. (Wayne "Dusty" Harris collection, FMM.)

Not content with being second best to the Medical Corps, the officers of HDLA and the 3rd Coast Artillery vied for the same musicians. In the 1941 Fort MacArthur Officers' Club orchestra, familiar faces can be seen, as many members played for the Fort MacArthur Band, the Officers' Club Orchestra, and the MEDICOS. Dusty Harris and few others even had their own after-hours band and played at local nightclubs. Harris recalls that he was making over $100 per week after hours. In 1941, privates earned $21 per month! (Wayne "Dusty" Harris collection, FMM: 1941.)

The Fort MacArthur Band also won great respect. Their history dated back to the 63rd Coast Artillery (AA) Regimental Band, which was considered by the garrison and the community as the best band in the army. Free Sunday afternoon concerts and weekly practice made them a huge hit with the locals. When the 63rd shipped out in December 1940, the entire band was transferred to the 3rd Coast Artillery. For a short time, noted conductor Leopold Stokowski, pictured here, led the band. Ralph Fetherolf (saxophone and clarinet) recalls that Stokowski was not popular with the troops because he did not understand the placement of army band members, preferring that of a normal orchestra. His tenure as bandleader was short-lived. (Gloria [Picazo] Rubio collection, FMM: 1941.)

With the new 3rd Coast Artillery Regiment trained and conditioned, the army sought to show off its expanded numbers in community events. Here Battery E, led by Capt. Harry J. "Hardrock" Harrison, marches through Beverly Hills. In appreciation of their participation, a local liquor store provided each soldier with two beers, and the troops were greeted by George Burns, Gracie Allen, and their children. Such was the support from the community in 1941. (Robert Rose collection, FMM.)

Soldiers were trained by the best the army had to offer, such as Battery E's top sergeant, Will J. Williams. Williams served with the 131st Infantry in World War I and was awarded the Distinguished Service Cross, Silver Star, and two Purple Hearts. He was a favorite with the soldiers, and after the outbreak of World War II, he was promoted directly to captain. He commanded Battery K, 3rd Coast Artillery. (Robert Rose collection, FMM: 1941.)

A weekend pass was something most soldiers eagerly anticipated. It was an opportunity to see local attractions and, for many, their first time to see an ocean beach. Pictured here in 1941 are Alexander Esparza (far left), Dick Shields (third from left), and two other members of Battery D at Cabrillo Beach. Esparza wears the Class A uniform, while the others wear their civilian clothes—a practice that was forbidden after December 7, 1941. Esparza was a boxer who, when inducted, was sent directly to Battery D without any basic training. The battery officers wanted the best boxer for the regimental matches. Esparza later went overseas and was decorated for his actions in the Philippines. (Guy R. "Dick" Shields collection, FMM.)

The Regimental Drum and Bugle Corps was comprised of soldiers from various batteries performing additional duty, such as Carl E. Bergstrom of Battery B. In 1941, the drums and bugles were outfitted in a red satin banner with gold fringe and the 3rd Coast Artillery insignia embroidered on it. (Carl E. Bergstrom collection, FMM.)

Soldiers' physical conditioning and stamina required development and maintenance. The coast artilleryman in full marching order is displayed by Pvt. John B. Sterrenberg of Swazy, Indiana, with a 1903 Springfield rifle, M1917A1 helmet, and a training gas mask. Curiously, he is wearing World War I–era leather reinforced leggings normally issued to mounted troops. (Robert Rose collection, FMM: 1941.)

The hills surrounding the fort were grueling for marches. Members of Headquarters Battery are in the process of a 25-mile march along the coastline, with numerous drills conducted along the way. Shortly after this c. 1941 photograph was taken, the men were ordered to wear their training masks for a portion of the march. (Earl J. Mohlke collection, FMM.)

No one was exempt from the marches. Pvt. Edward T. (Tom) Tregilgas models the full marching order for members of the 3rd Coast Artillery Band, complete with a World War I–era M1917 helmet and ball peen hammer in the bayonet strap on his pack. Ralph Fetherolf, the photographer, recalls that band members were issued only .45-caliber pistols for their weapons and without the butt of a rifle "had nothing to drive in the tent stakes so we took the hammers." (Ralph I. Fetherolf collection, FMM: 1941.)

Cpl. Danver Withrow and Pvt. Red Hendren of Battery E show off their canvas home for the night. In some cases, troops were left overnight at the BES. Tents were the only shelter other than the stations themselves. (Robert Rose collection, FMM.)

In June 1941, workers at the North American Aviation plant in Inglewood went on strike. The strike was fueled by labor advocates and became unruly. Batteries B and E, 3rd Coast Artillery were ordered to Inglewood to break the strike. The troops line up just prior to their departure for Inglewood. (Earl Mohlke collection, FMM.)

The North American Aviation Plant is seen in background as elements of Battery E prepare to march on the strikers. Bob Rose recalls, "We were issued live ammunition and our weapons were locked and loaded. This was no fooling around." When the soldiers advanced, there were some fights and at least one striker was butt-stroked with a rifle while another jabbed in the buttocks with a bayonet. The strike ended in two hours. The incident was featured in a June 1941 issue of *Life* magazine. Some sources only credit the 15th Infantry as participating in this labor strike action. The Battery E guidon (flag) clearly positioned in this photograph should leave no doubt of the presence of the coast artillery. Fort MacArthur troops claim that the infantry showed up later and that the coast artillerymen were in the lead. The Winchester trench gun in the right foreground suggests that this was a fairly serious crowd control operation. (Robert Rose collection, FMM.)

An additional weapon was introduced into the fort's defenses in 1941—the K-9 Corps. Fort MacArthur seems to have been the first army post to develop an active K-9 Command that was incorporated into daily operations of the garrison. K-9 Corps operations were expanded into all of HDLA. This 1941 photograph shows Pvt. Hershel Adams of Battery A grooming a Fort MacArthur canine detailed to guard a BES. (FMM.)

With its proximity to Hollywood, many Fort MacArthur soldiers were starstruck. One soldier from Battery B, Fred McClintock, was so starstruck that he commented that he would like to eat Thanksgiving dinner with Jane Wyman. Following severe badgering by the men of the battery, McClintock was forced to "put up" or "shut up." He went to Warner Brothers Studios and made his way in to meet Miss Wyman. After explaining his predicament, Miss Wyman agreed to dinner and McClintock won the bet with the crew. On November 20, 1941, Sgt. Arthur Dahlstein, Battery B's top sergeant, is carving the turkey at an Upper Reservation Mess Hall. (International News photograph, FMM.)

Five

WAR, THE YARDBIRDS, AND THE SERVICE COMMAND

"We are all in this war, every man, woman, and child," exclaimed President Roosevelt during his announcement on December 8. The fort that had enjoyed such growth with new troops was now considered in a theater of operation. Remote gun positions were manned, daily alerts mounted, and weapons drills occupied the time. Many of the draftees of the previous year, who had missed their separation by weeks and in some cases by mere days, were now in for the duration. These men were suddenly the old timers ready to train new recruits. In addition to its fighting role, the fort continued to induct servicemen. The fort also developed new morale-boosting entertainment operations as part of a newly identified role on the home front. Perhaps the most significant entertainment operation conducted by the fort was the *Hey Rookie* program. Originally developed to boost the morale of troops stationed at remote harbor defense locations, the show became an instant hit. It was selected for a public viewing in Long Beach and received even more praise. It was such a hit that a theater in downtown Los Angeles was secured, and the show played to sold-out audiences for nearly nine months! At the conclusion of its downtown run, the program was selected to go overseas in order to maintain morale of allied troops. The proximity of Hollywood and the large number of people employed in the entertainment industry gave the fort a curious mix of new recruits. Sensing the value of the entertainment industry draftees, the fort soon secured musicians, set designers, writers, composers, caterers, cartoonists, and countless other entertainment types. Sensing the dubious combat value of some of these men, the fort's special services command grew and augmented the coast defense force by providing morale-boosting events throughout greater Los Angeles. As the war progressed, elements of the 9th Service Command at Fort MacArthur played a more significant role by operating the induction center "round the clock" and shipping men out for service overseas. The coast artillery maintained its important role and even received newer and more powerful weaponry. Ultimately the war was an overseas business and many of the garrison rotated out for overseas service. By war's end, 750,000 soldiers had been processed at Fort MacArthur.

For men of the fort, Sunday, December 7, 1941, began as a fairly regular day. The band was assigned to perform a public concert at Camp Seaside in Ventura. Cpl. Roy Wilde and Pvts. Harold Blackburn and Howard Williams face the camera in the back of a one and half ton Chevrolet cargo truck during the early morning drive to Ventura. (Wayne "Dusty" Harris collection, FMM.)

At the conclusion of the concert, band members met local dignitaries and personalities. Pictured here, from left to right, are Pvt. Royce Woolery, Pfc. Paul Tompkins, Pfc. Dusty Harris, Carmen Camarillo, warrant officer Rudolph Klenik (band leader), unidentified, Pfc. Claude Chidley, Sgt. George Thams, Ivan Parker (attorney), unidentified, Pvt. Lloyd Lunham, and Pvt. Howard Williams. (Wayne "Dusty" Harris collection, FMM.)

The band had lunch at Camp Seaside shortly before the news of the Japanese attack at Pearl Harbor. When they learned the news, the band immediately loaded into the trucks and quickly returned to Fort MacArthur with an escort from the highway patrol. (Wayne "Dusty" Harris collection, FMM.)

Almost instantly, Fort MacArthur geared up for war, as can be seen on Pacific Avenue looking south from the band barracks. Peacetime regulations were supplanted with restrictive wartime measures, and many residents were restricted in access to their homes when the barricades went up. Some were even ordered to leave for the duration. Many band members had frequented the Green Spot Cafe (in the background), but it was placed off limits immediately after Pearl Harbor. The Green Spot ultimately became a favorite again once restrictions were relaxed. (Ralph Fetherolf collection, FMM: December 8, 1941.)

Defensive measures were established at the gate on Pacific Avenue between Twenty-fourth and Twenty-sixth Streets, formerly the main gate. During the war, the main gate was moved to Twenty-eighth Street and Pacific Avenue. (FMM: December 10, 1941.)

Changes to the landscape of the fort included slit trenches dug near barracks and buildings. The "trees" near the trenches are believed to be posts for camouflage netting that had not yet been placed. (Howard Schroeder collection, FMM: c. December 1941.)

Differently designed slit trenches were emplaced near the barracks on the Middle Reservation. Zigzag trenches had the same purpose as box side trenches—to limit the lethal effects of shrapnel if the trench took a direct hit. (Howard Schroeder collection, FMM: *c.* December 1941.)

The canines of Fort MacArthur were a more common sight after the war began. Here Al Robles kneels with a member of the K-9 Command in front of the headquarters building. Shortly after Pearl Harbor, in December 1941, the basement windows of the building were sandbagged as part of the air raid precautions. The basement housed important administrative offices and was occupied by numerous soldiers and civilian employees. (Earl Mohlke collection, FMM.)

Increased wartime activity also occurred on the Lower Reservation. In addition to housing the busy reception center, Bottomside was the site of the HDLA motor pool and Battery A with the 14-inch railway guns. Robert Hogarth was one of two BAR (Browning Automatic Rifle) men in Battery A. In the background are some rarely seen support cars for the railway guns. (Robert Hogarth collection, FMM: c. 1942.)

The Lower Reservation also had dugouts for air raid attacks, such as this sandbagged shelter with Earl Mohlke in front in December 1941. These bluffs separate the Middle and Lower Reservations. (Earl Mohlke collection, FMM.)

Topside defenses were improved by the construction of trenches and fighting positions. Pvt. William Ayers occupies a position with his BAR in one of the Topside trenches in 1942. Remnants of some trenches are still visible at Battery Osgood-Farley, which currently houses the Fort MacArthur Museum. (FMM.)

In 1942, Ayers poses with a BAR near a camouflaged gun battery. According to Charles Short from Battery D, the first camouflage nets had no burlap in them. Troops were ordered to shred old socks and clothing to weave through the nets to better camouflage the guns. (FMM.)

With war came the requirements that nearly every position had to be manned around the clock. For gun crews, this meant bunking inside the batteries. For the fire control and observation crews, it meant bunking near the BES. In Battery A, Pvt. Donald Hanna was one of the observers. He and a few other men were ordered to bunk in the stations, making the BES far too crowded. They ultimately built an underground shelter near the stations using wood, cables, and other materials seen in this photograph. (Donald Hanna collection, FMM: *c.* 1942.)

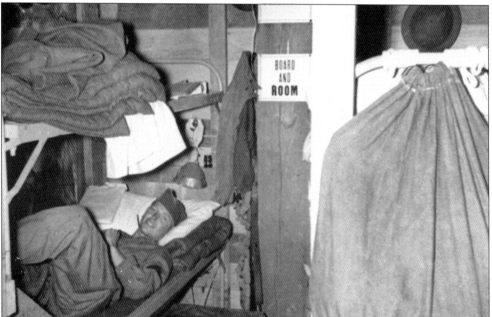

This underground room became home for a while, and the men brought everything they might need to the shelter. Around 1942, Cpl. John Kinchloe takes a break in one of the bunks. In the 1980s, this site was uncovered during a city park expansion project. Inside was a paper name tag affixed to a wall that read "Hanna." The tag and the door from the structure are part of the museum's collection. (Donald Hanna collection, FMM.)

Many remote positions existed on the coast. Here, in December 1941, men from Batteries B and E are adding the final touches and camouflage to Battery Tucker at Long Point, named unofficially by the men for their former commander, who had died the previous year. Immediately after news of the Pearl Harbor attack, Battery B with elements of Battery E, adhering to prewar plans, began moving two 155 GPFs to Long Point. The crosshairs taped on the muzzle of this 155 GPF is believed to be some form of bore sight. (Selma [Harrison] Calmes collection, FMM.)

Capt. Harry (Hardrock) Harrison meets with an enlisted man from the 265th Coast Artillery Regiment at the Long Point 155 position. The 2nd Battalion of the 265th arrived on December 11, 1941, to relieve Batteries B and E of the assignment at Long Point. The 265th was a Florida National Guard unit that had moved to Fort Crockett, Texas. After the Pearl Harbor attack, the unit was relocated to Fort MacArthur to augment its defenses. (Selma [Harrison] Calmes collection, FMM.)

Reinforcements were also received from the 78th Coast Artillery (Anti-Aircraft). Battery G was stationed at the Lakewood Golf Course with a three-inch gun positioned near Tee No. 1. Sgt. John Ljutich and an unidentified soldier of Battery G (wearing breeches) are patrolling near the gun on December 7. Both are wearing World War I cartridge belts and M1917A1 helmets. (John V. Ljutich collection, FMM.)

The beaches in Orange County were also defended. This camouflaged emplacement in Bolsa Chica was part of Battery B. Construction features included chicken wire net secured by turnbuckles. In the early part of the war, all available resources were used to camouflage positions. (Arthur Earick collection, FMM: c. 1942.)

This very rare aerial view of the Upper Reservation shows some of the camouflage measures employed at the fort. This image, taken in 1943, shows the almost invisible Batteries Osgood-Farley and Leary-Merriam. Some trenches are visible in the center of the photograph. The six-inch Battery 241 under construction is visible in the right center of the photograph, while the Middle and Lower Reservations are visible in the upper left corner. (W. W. Hicks collection, FMM.)

Within weeks of the Pearl Harbor attack, Fort MacArthur and San Pedro got their first taste of the war. At 10:30 a.m. on December 24, two miles off Point Fermin, the freighter *Absaroka* was torpedoed by the Japanese submarine I-19. The ship was loaded with lumber and therefore remained afloat. This photograph was taken through the DPF scope at the Sea Bench BES for Battery Osgood-Farley by Sgt. Dick Shields, just minutes after the attack. (Dick Shields collection, FMM.)

The *Absaroka* was towed into Los Angeles Harbor and ultimately repaired. This image of the stricken ship was taken from the Lower Reservation on the afternoon of December 24. (Earl Mohlke collection, FMM.)

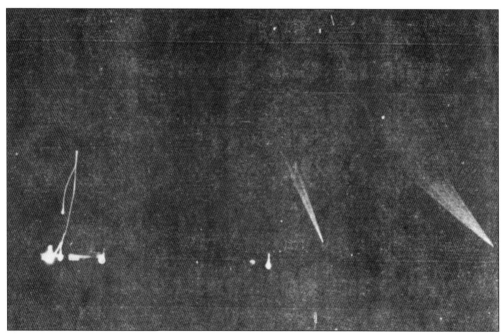

Another scare for the fort came in the early morning of February 25, 1942. As enemy aircraft were reportedly approaching Los Angeles, air raid sirens blared, searchlights swept the sky, and ultimately anti-aircraft guns opened fire. No one knows the precise details, but some eyewitnesses will swear to this day that there were aircraft in the sky while others claim they saw no aircraft at all. Despite the lack of details, the event is often called the "L.A. Air Raid." This image captures some of the searchlights and anti-aircraft fire from that night. (Associated Press photograph, FMM.)

The day after the air raid was spent assessing damage and disposing of unexploded ordnance. Officer B. H. McClean and Lt. E. D. Dillard keep people away from a possible bomb. No enemy bombs were discovered, though. These were anti-aircraft shells that failed to detonate. (*Los Angeles Herald Express* photograph, FMM.)

Even before President Roosevelt's executive order to remove all persons of Japanese ancestry from the West Coast, Fort MacArthur troops were sent to enforce the removal of the Japanese (American citizens and non-citizens) from Terminal Island. Some troops felt the removal was a good idea; others regretted the decision, having made friends among the local farmers and fishermen. (*Los Angeles Times* photograph, FMM: February 24, 1942.)

The threat of sabotage was a major concern for the fort. The Fort MacArthur K-9 Command augmented nightly patrols of the areas surrounding the fort, as seen here in spring 1942. Far from being simply guard dogs, these canines served a variety of defensive functions. (FMM.)

While the permanent troops of the fort and the HDLA were engaged in preparation for combat, the reception center shifted into full speed and operated around the clock. Hundreds of thousands of men were processed here by war's end. In 1942, this new inductee takes a look at one of Uncle Sam's newest GIs at the Fort MacArthur Reception Center. (Gloria [Picazo] Rubio collection, FMM.)

New equipment made it to the permanent troops, such as new M1 helmets that arrived at Fort MacArthur in the summer of 1942. These soldiers are manning a concrete and brick anti-aircraft fighting position Topside. They are posing with a Browning M1917A1 water-cooled machine gun on an improvised anti-aircraft mount. A few of these positions remain on the Upper Reservation along Gaffey Street. (FMM.)

Certain aspects of fort life remained the same. Morning wake up by the "Charge of Quarters" was a daily routine. This 1942 photograph may have been posed, but it still provides an idea of a typical wake-up call. (FMM.)

Army mess procedures changed with the outbreak of hostilities. Previously the army provided money directly to each battery mess sergeant, who purchased food directly. As the war progressed, food was centrally procured and issued to each battery. This is the post's butcher shop around 1943, where meat was divided up for each battery. Above the counters surrounding the cutting blocks are plaques listing the various batteries supplied by the fort, under which the batteries' cuts are stacked. (Gloria [Picazo] Rubio collection, FMM.)

This image shows some of the most important men in the battery—mess cooks. (These are from Battery K.) Officers and enlisted men alike could tell the quality of a battery's food by the morale of the men. Pictured, from left to right, are (first row) Mitchell Nytko and Technician 4th Grade Gore; (second row) Sergeant Duncan, Tidor Simosik, A. G. Morici, John Coyne, and W. R. Shepard. Note the method of posting menus, regulations, and the number of soldiers served. (Earl Dill collection, FMM.)

Victory gardens were a common site at the fort. Mess sergeants and battery members often sought to augment rations with homegrown fruits and vegetables. In 1943, Earl Mohlke tends the Headquarters Battery victory garden on Twenty-first Street just outside the Fort MacArthur Twenty-second Street gate. (Earl Mohlke collection, FMM.)

As the war progressed, some of the earlier restrictions were lifted, including the prohibition against purchasing lunch off post. Millie Wheeler, seen here in 1942, was the local waitress at the Green Spot Cafe who captured the heart of Sgt. Dick Shields. They were married in September 1943. (Dick Shields collection, FMM.)

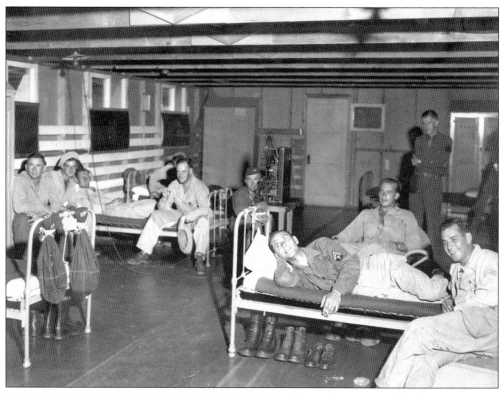

Entertainment was also important for the troops' morale. In 1942, the men of Battery K enjoy a film in their barracks. Footwear is properly laid out under early model Quartermaster bed frames that date from the early 1900s. (Earl Dill collection, FMM.)

Early in the war, Sgt. Johnny Walker recognized the sinking morale of the soldiers at the fort. News from the front—Pearl Harbor, Wake Island, the Philippines, and the Bataan Death March—was almost all bad. (Many Fort MacArthur troops had been transferred to the Philippines in early 1941.) Walker, a World War I veteran, came up with a plan to build a mobile entertainment group called the Yardbirds. With approval from Colonel Hicks, Walker formed the Fort MacArthur Yardbirds and began his morale-boosting campaign. (Wayne "Dusty" Harris collection, FMM.)

Some of the first volunteers for the program were members of the 3rd Coast Artillery Band. These talented musicians would provide the backbone for Yardbird performances. Ralph Fetherolf (first row, fifth from left) served with the Yardbirds from beginning to end. (Ralph Fetherolf collection, FMM: *c.* 1942.)

Walker and the Yardbirds were able to secure a trailer and materials to build a mobile stage. This is the completed stage in towing configuration, complete with the Roger insignia of the Yardbirds, *c.* 1942. The term yardbird usually applied to new soldiers that weren't exactly sure what to do in any given situation. (Ralph Fetherolf collection, FMM.)

In 1942, this is the open trailer with band members in place. This photograph, taken at one of the earliest performances, shows various music stands and the 3rd Coast Artillery Regiment crest painted on the mural at the back of the stage. (Ralph Fetherolf collection, FMM.)

In addition to the band, there were other performers and acts. Here "Adolph" gets a wallop from one of the fort's officers. All performers had regular duties with the various batteries and were expected to perform with the Yardbirds in addition to those responsibilities. (Ralph Fetherolf collection, FMM.)

The Yardbirds were so successful that they were presented to the general public with great acclaim. As the show developed, its name was changed to *Hey Rookie* starring the Fort MacArthur Yardbirds. With increasing success, each member was issued a certificate. President Roosevelt was made an honorary Yardbird and was presented with a certificate and a statuette of Roger, which reportedly remained on his desk until his death in 1945. (Wayne "Dusty" Harris collection, FMM: *c.* 1943.)

Hey Rookie became so popular that a permanent theater, the Belasco in Los Angeles, was secured for its performances. The show also gained some notable stars, including actor Sterling Holloway in the lead role. Here, around 1943, Sterling Holloway enjoys rapturous tunes during one of the skits. (Gloria [Picazo] Rubio collection, FMM.)

Some members of the *Hey Rookie* team must have had the most unusual duties ever assigned to coast artillerymen. Kermit French of Battery C was in charge of ticket sales for the show. Although an accomplished coast artilleryman (attested by the "E" for excellence patch on his right cuff), he and Cpl. Newman Nervig were assigned to a room in the Embassy Hotel in order to be near the Belasco. French poses here at the entrance of the Belasco Theater. (Kermit French collection, FMM.)

Edward "Duney" Truax had numerous roles throughout the show. Here, in 1943, he performs "Jenny the Jeep" with Sterling Holloway as the voice of the Jeep. While *Hey Rookie* operated in Los Angeles, it was always connected with the 3rd Coast Artillery rather than the 9th Service Command or other branches of the army, making it a very unique operation. (FMM.)

Hey Rookie was extremely successful and ran for nearly nine months at the Belasco. Some of the biggest names in Hollywood attended performances and supported the program. Here actresses Anita Louise and Claudette Colbert accompany Col. W. W. Hicks, an unidentified major general, and an unidentified female guest to one of the performances, *c.* 1943. In the background on the right are Sterling Holloway and Adolph Monjou. (FMM.)

Next door to the Belasco was the Mayan Theater and both shared a common alley. During breaks in the performances or rehearsals, casts from shows at the Mayan joined the *Hey Rookie* crew for fun and games. Actor Ed Wynn entertains the casts with readings from a favorite book, *c.* 1943. (FMM.)

The finale of the show involved a mass formation on the stage led by Johnny Walker singing "Wake Up America." At the end of the show's run, army brass decided it had been so successful that it would be sent to entertain troops overseas. (FMM: c. 1943.)

Hey Rookie brought new wealth to the Fort MacArthur recreation fund. Over $350,000 was generated and some of the revenue built the Hey Rookie swimming pools. On July 14, 1944, the Southern California Aquabelles perform a synchronized formation spelling U.S. at the Hey Rookie Pool No. 2, Topside. After this performance, the Aquabelles became an instant hit and ended up performing throughout the region to raise money for the seventh war loan. (Jean [Dobbs] Schopp collection, FMM.)

The Aquabelles performances in the *Hey Rookie* pool were called Aquacades and were always a big hit with the troops. Over 2,000 people attended this performance, making the pool one of San Pedro's largest outdoor venues. Sadly the pool has suffered from years of neglect and vandalism with almost no thought given to its origins and the role that it played during World War II. Most people don't even know its proper name. (Jean [Dobbs] Schopp collection, FMM.)

Morale-boosting activities were not limited to *Hey Rookie*. As the war progressed, leading women personalities from Hollywood formed the Volunteer Army Canteen Service (VACS). The VACS were reportedly the only civilian organization with a permanent status on any military reservation in the country. They operated three canteens on post that were stunning successes. Here the Topside canteen hosts members of the *Hey Rookie* cast, c. 1943. (FMM.)

The VACS were so treasured that a formal parade was authorized in their honor. The VACS commitment to the fort is evident in this 1943 photograph. Many notable names were found on the VACS roster, including Claudette Colbert, Anita Louise, Barbara Stanwyck, Mrs. Louis B. Mayer, Mildred Knopf, and Mrs. Jack Benny. (Gloria [Picazo] Rubio collection, FMM.)

The success of *Hey Rookie*, the VACS, and the Aquabelles brought the Special Services office, traditionally staffed by coast artillery personnel, new prominence in the administration of the fort. As Special Services gained recognition, their operations were transferred to the 9th Service Command, but distinctions between the two offices were often blurred. From left to right are Lupe Saldana, Gloria Picazo, Bobbeye McIntyre, four unidentified Service Command members, Emil (Zeke) Zekely, and Howard Young of the Service Command. It's December 1943, and they are stuffing envelopes containing *Hey Rookie* souvenir booklets, Chesterfield cigarettes, Baby Ruth candy bars, and a special wallet for every member of HDLA. (Gloria [Picazo] Rubio collection, FMM.)

Some of the morale-boosting operations of the Service Command were more subtle. Here members of the True Blue Club dump their black books to stay true to their boyfriends overseas. Pictured, from left to right, are unidentified, Elaine Miniger, and Bobbye McIntyre. These civilians are wearing special dark blue uniforms with the 9th Service Command patch. Colonel Hicks ordered the civilians to purchase these uniforms and wear them while on duty. The order was later cancelled by a higher authority. (Bobbye [McIntyre] Sweny collection, FMM.)

One of the most important operations of the 9th Service Command was hosting the visit of Mexican president Manuel Avila Camacho. Mexico declared war on the Axis powers in June 1942, and the president visited the fort as a new ally. This photograph of one of the events shows an extremely rare glimpse of one of the 14-inch railway guns in its special shelter made to look like an ordinary barracks building. (Gloria [Picazo] Rubio collection, FMM.)

Emil (Zeke) Zekely was one of the Service Command's best assets. Zeke was a talented cartoonist working for Ed McManus on the syndicated *Maggie and Jiggs* cartoon strip. He was drafted and assigned as the cartoonist for the *Fort MacArthur Alert*, the post's weekly newspaper. Famous for his lovely caricatures of women, he became an instant success with the troops. (Gloria [Picazo] Rubio collection, FMM: *c.* 1944.)

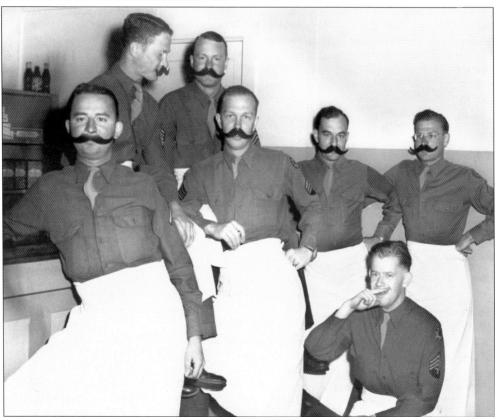

While some of Special Services' functions were more subtle than others, they still had some effect on morale. Here Jack Cleland (kneeling) and the staff of the Silver Dollar Red Room Bar prepare for its last day of operation in Middleside. The bar had been a tremendous hit with the men and was soon reopened at the Lower Reservation. (Gloria [Picazo] Rubio collection, FMM: 1943.)

Despite losing many of its members to the *Hey Rookie* show when it transferred overseas, the 3rd Coast Artillery Band still performed at the fort and throughout the southland. Tech. Sgt. Stanley Clark describes his decorations to a Salvation Army member after a band performance. Clark saw action with Pershing in Mexico and in Siberia after World War I. (Stanley Clark collection, FMM.)

As the threat from attack diminished, some coast artillery units performed in Service Command events. In 1944, members of Battery K illuminated the skies above the Los Angeles Coliseum with their Sperry M1941 searchlights. The large, rotating color wheel was used to make a spectacular show of lights. (Earl Dill collection, FMM.)

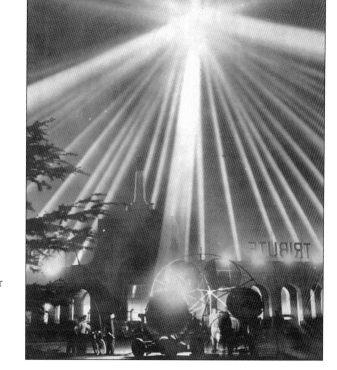

The coliseum light show was seen from the San Gabriel Mountains around 1944. These spectacular shows were often conducted during peacetime but had not been seen since the outbreak of hostilities. (Dan Eagle collection, FMM.)

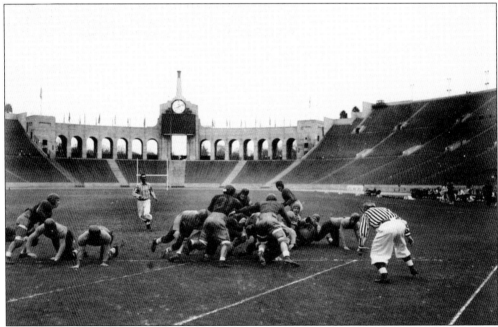

In 1944, the Cannoneers, the Fort MacArthur football team, made their appearance. Staffed entirely by men of the coast artillery, the team had remarkable success. Coach Gene Clark, a USC All American player, and quarterback Ned Matthews, a UCLA All American, led the team to victory as they beat both USC and UCLA's second teams. They were defeated only once, by the San Diego Naval Training Station team, which was primarily made up of professional athletes drafted by the navy. Veterans recall that everyone who played in San Diego got hurt! (Doug Wall collection, FMM.)

A new gymnasium and equipment purchased from *Hey Rookie* proceeds enabled the fort to develop quite an athletics program. Battery D's basketball team, from left to right, included (first row) Carl Fox, Joseph Caravana, and Thurmond Siders; (second row) Noble Clements, William Bailey, Dick Shields, and ? Thorne. (Dick Shields collection, FMM.)

Due to tremendous strides made by Special Services on the morale front, coast artillery crews remained at peak efficiency. Battery G manned a three-inch M1903 rapid-fire seacoast gun on Cabrillo Beach with Sgt. Manual Ramos leading the crew. Pictured around 1943, from left to right, are Sgt. Ramos, Pvt. Johnson, Cpl. Floyd Lee, Pvt. Dempsy, Pvt. Houseneck, Pvt. Morris, and Pvt. Cabria. (Everett Sweny collection, FMM.)

Regular practice was required to keep gun crews at high readiness. The P-12 target tow craft hauled distant targets for practice firing. Boat crews often spoke vividly of the rough seas and questioned the survivability of the P-12. She brought the men back every time, however. (Howard Schroeder collection, FMM: c. 1943.)

Gun commanders and the battery commander of Battery A, 522nd Coast Artillery Battalion (formerly Battery C, 3rd Coast Artillery) admire the results of a very successful shoot. Battery A manned the six-inch guns of Battery 240 in Palos Verdes. This April 1945 practice was a gun commander's action, meaning that the fire control was conducted directly by the gun crew. (Dick Shields collection, FMM.)

Smaller guns were used as part of the Anti Motor Torpedo Boat (AMTB) batteries. In 1944, men from Battery G manned this 40-mm gun at the Long Beach AMTB Battery, which was also used for anti-aircraft defense. (Everett Sweny collection, FMM.)

On May 22, 1944, Battery G had the most tragic accident of the war at the fort. During a 90-mm AMTB gun-firing drill, one of the crewmembers dropped a shell on its nose. The shells were armed with point detonating fuses and the projectile exploded, killing one and seriously wounding eight others. These are members of the gun crew involved in the accident. (Doug Wall collection, FMM.)

The accident also produced the only decoration for heroism at the fort during the war. Doug Wall, a crewman on the gun, noticed that a ready shell had been pierced by fragments from the detonated shell and was smoldering. He picked up the shell, carried it to the water's edge, and threw it into the sea. For his actions, he was awarded the Soldier's Medal in 1944. Colonel Hicks awarded the medal to Wall, while in the background accepting the Purple Heart are the parents of Pfc. Robert Fox, the soldier who perished in the accident. (Doug Wall collection, FMM.)

Updated armament arrived in the form of Battery 127—two 16-inch guns built on the hillside above White's Point, west of the Upper Reservation. These tremendous weapons had greater range and were also controlled by radar. The battery was later named after Col. Paul D. Bunker, who was starved to death by the Japanese after being captured on Corregidor. He had served at the fort and was a very popular officer. (Dick Shields collection, FMM: 1944.)

The seriousness of firing practices was tempered with some fun as well. Members of the medical detachment at the 155 Battery at Playa Del Rey prepare to dispense "medicinal" alcohol for the members of the detachment and have used the ambulance to transport the keg. Pictured around 1944, from left to right, are Frank Yoder, Randall Hatch, Frank Bowser, Richard Ruff, and Mike Hahn. (Richard Ruff collection, FMM.)

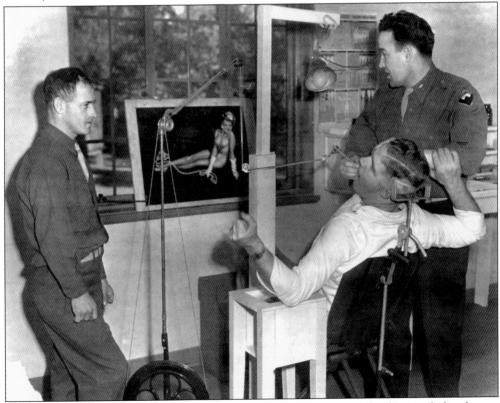

Garrison daily routine continued at the fort, but the troops were never shy about including humor into the situation, such as this dentist being "distracted" while drilling on a hapless patient. The new Western Defense Command shoulder patch worn by the dentist was introduced in late 1944. (Dan Eagle collection, FMM.)

The pistol range at the base of Battery Osgood-Farley was the site of small arms qualification for soldiers with Thompson M1928 and M1 submachine guns. This is the same area that was used by units in the 1920s and 1930s, only with a new structure. (Dan Eagle collection, FMM: c. 1944.)

In late 1944, training shifted emphasis to preparing soldiers for overseas deployment. The war was moving farther away from the U.S. mainland, so training was modified. Soldiers learned swimming and survival techniques at the *Hey Rookie* pool No. 2, Topside. (Dan Eagle collection, FMM.)

As more troops trained and deployed for overseas duty, even the K-9 Command gave up a valued leader. Bob Pearce, now a warrant officer, was transferred to the Pacific. In 1943, Pearce is pictured with Rin Tin Tin III at the Upper Reservation kennel and training area. The K-9 Command that Pearce built continued to serve the fort into the postwar years. (Gloria [Picazo] Rubio collection, FMM.)

Even the venerable Clark brothers, Stanley and James, were not spared from transfer. They show off their stripes and hash marks after transferring to the Los Angeles Port of Embarkation. Together the Clark brothers gave more that 59 years of service to the army, many with the 3rd and 63rd Coast Artillery Bands. The family (father and three sons) accumulated more than 135 years service by the end of 1945. (James Clark collection, FMM.)

On July 24, 1945, Col. W. W. Hicks left the post. He was awarded the Legion of Merit by Maj. Gen. Walter Wilson for his meritorious achievements shortly after the outbreak of hostilities. Colonel Hicks successfully provided logistics support for a force of over 30,000 men with an organization that was geared to supply a peacetime garrison of 2,000. (Dan Eagle collection, FMM.)

Major General Wilson toasts with other members of the Fort MacArthur staff on V-J Day in 1945. Many of these men would be discharged within the next few months, while some would stay and carry on the new activities of the peacetime garrison. (Dan Eagle collection, FMM.)

Six

POSTWAR POSSIBILITIES AND NIKE

After the war, the fort continued to process soldiers for return to civilian life. Concurrently the coast defense forces were significantly reduced and many of the fixed emplacement weapons were scrapped. As the nation eagerly delved into peacetime existence, army planners sensed that this would be an uneasy peace. Army leaders knew there would again be need for trained soldiers and began new programs for the Organized Reserve Corps (ORC). ORC activities at the fort brought men from every branch of the army—armor, infantry, engineers, and other—and they all gathered at various times throughout the year. The permanent garrison, after a relative period of calm, experienced some profound changes. In 1950, the fort was considered for a change to an amphibious engineer base. This was a short-term experiment that gave way to a more permanent garrison charged with the Air Defense of Los Angeles. The army introduced the Nike missile defense system in 1954, and Fort MacArthur became the headquarters of the Los Angeles Air Defense Command. Originally equipped with Nike Ajax missiles manned by regular army troops, the system went through constant modifications and improvements resulting in one of the most advanced air defense systems in the world equipped with the nuclear capable Nike Hercules. Throughout the Nike era, members of the California National Guard shared the air defense role with the regular army. The Fort MacArthur National Guardsmen were amongst the finest in the country and left a tremendous legacy for the fort and the National Guard when the Nike system was shut down in 1974.

At the end of the war, Fort MacArthur shifted from its role of an induction center to that of a separation center. During the sometimes lengthy separation process, outgoing troops were billeted wherever space was available. In 1946, the fort received a special visit from General Eisenhower, who chatted with outgoing troops at the Lower Reservation. The sergeant at left already has his Ruptured Duck patch sewn above his right shirt pocket and has his records packet in his hands. (FMM.)

The Organized Reserve Corps (ORC) used the fort for a variety of purposes, but one of the more obvious changes came from the 45th Medium Tank Battalion, whose M4A3E8 Shermans arrived in 1949. The battalion's headquarters was in Pasadena, but the tanks and most of the training was conducted at Fort MacArthur. Pvt. Ray Curtis is receiving instructions from M. Sgt. Robert Jeffs on the exterior telephone system of the tank in 1949, as Pvt. Albert Morse watches with amusement. The 13th Armored Division patches are positioned over their left pockets and placed on their helmet liners. (Albert Morse collection, FMM.)

The main gate remained on Pacific Avenue in early 1950. These peacetime security measures are a marked contrast to those employed after December 7, 1941. The Jeep's bumper is painted "Fort MacArthur." (Mike Mewkalo collection, FMM.)

This is the Fort MacArthur Post Exchange in 1950. During ORC cycles, the PX was quite busy, but otherwise, peacetime operations were flat. When the Korean War broke out, the fort resumed a busy schedule providing training and mustering facilities for troops shipping out for Korea. (Mike Mewkalo collection, FMM.)

In contrast to the relative calm of the fort in the immediate postwar years, *Hey Rookie* pool No. 2 was quite busy. The army opened it for public use, and hundreds of San Pedro kids learned to swim in this great pool that was a community gathering place for decades. Pictured in 1946, from left to right, are Emma Alsaker, unidentified, Hilda Hansen, unidentified, Allen Alsaker, Dorothy Lund, Alan Lund, and unidentified at the water's edge. (Dorothy (Lund) Matich collection, FMM.)

In October 1950, the conversion of the fort into an amphibious engineer base began with the arrival of 3,000 men with the 409th Engineer Amphibious Special Brigade over a three-day period. The 380th Boat Maintenance Battalion (part of the 409th EASB) headquarters building on the Lower Reservation displays the amphibious engineers insignia and guidon. The insignia was affectionately called the "pregnant worm." (Emmett Drennen collection, FMM.)

In 1950, Capt. Emmett Drennen, commanding officer of Company D, 380th Boat Maintenance Battalion and an unidentified warrant officer pose near the LCM-6's of the 409th EASB at Fort MacArthur. After only 11 months, the brigade was partially deactivated and various units were dispersed throughout the army, with some going straight to Korea. This marked the end of the amphibious engineers at Fort MacArthur. (Emmett Drennen collection, FMM.)

Movie stars continued to visit Fort MacArthur in the postwar years. Abbott and Costello visited WACS in a mess facility in December 1955 and chatted with, from left to right, unidentified, Private Omes, Lou Costello, Private Hullum, and Bud Abbott. The WACS are wearing the taupe uniform with the 6th Army patch. It was introduced in the early 1950s to replace the OD uniform. (FMM.)

On September 12, 1960, Capt. Pat Centacessi briefs Japanese officers on the Nike Ajax missiles at the Brea launch site (LA-29). By the end of the Korean War, the requirement for coast artillery and anti-aircraft gun units was decreasing and the army replaced these with air defense missile units. In the mid-1950s, headquarters for the Air Defense Artillery in Los Angeles came to the fort. The Los Angeles system had 16 sites during the Cold War. (Aralas Ross collection, FMM.)

A fueling demonstration was performed by members of D Battery, 554th Missile Battalion at the Point Vincente site (LA-55) in September 1956. One of the most dangerous aspects of the Nike Ajax missile was its liquid fuel. The fuel was so caustic that it could eat through skin. It was highly combustible, requiring elaborate safety measures during fueling operations. (Lyle Jordan collection, FMM.)

The missile troops used the Integrated Fire Control (IFC) to first acquire the target and then track both the target and the missile. The IFC for the Fort MacArthur Nike site (LA-43) was on Topside. The launch site was to the west at White Point near the former 16-inch gun position, Battery Bunker. Around 1970, various radar domes on the former Merriam-Leary 14-inch gun battery are seen in the upper left center. Battery Osgood-Farley is to the right center. (FMM.)

This is one of many public exhibits of the new Nike Hercules (Herc) missile on the Middle Reservation. In the late 1950s, the army began upgrading the Nike Ajax missiles with the Nike Hercules system. The Herc was a larger missile capable of being armed with a nuclear warhead. It also had solid fuel rocket engines not requiring the hazardous fueling process of the Ajax. (Aralas Ross collection, FMM: c. 1960.)

The "Blue Room" interior of the Nike missile control room was located underground on the Middle Reservation. The later Ajax batteries and the new Hercules system had a more advanced fire control system called Missile Master that connected all of the firing batteries in the Los Angeles basin. It could acquire and track more targets and controlled launch at all the batteries. (Homer Pountious collection, FMM: c. 1962.)

The cast of *The Dick Van Dyke Show* pose with members of Fort Mac Arthur's 47th Air Defense Artillery Brigade demonstrating Hollywood's support of the Nike program. In the early 1960s, both Ajax and Hercules missiles were transported to various public relations events throughout Southern California. (Aralas Ross collection, FMM.)

In 1965, Specialist Jesse Aguilar, D Battery, 4th Battalion, 251st Artillery (CNG) poses with his canine Excel at the White Point kennel and training area. The fort's K-9 Command and the Army K-9 Corps were virtually disbanded in the late 1940s and early 1950s, only to return to Los Angles in November 1958. As many of the Nike sites were located in remote areas, the army decided that canines should be used to aid in defending the sites. Aguilar is wearing his belt buckle reversed to keep the buckle from being scratched by a pistol belt, thus preserving the polish for inspections. (Jesse Aguilar collection, FMM.)

A Nike Herc missile is on the launcher at the White Point launch site (LA-43), manned by Battery D, 4th Missile Battalion, 251st Air Defense Artillery (CNG). In 1957, the 720th Missile Battalion (Nike Ajax) became the first National Guard unit to be designated as a missile unit. In 1962, the battalion was redesignated the 4th Missile Battalion (Nike Hercules), 251st Artillery (CNG). In June 1966, Battery D scored a perfect rating on their Short Notice Annual Practice (SNAP) drill becoming the first unit in the continental U.S. to achieve a perfect score. The canine kennel and training area is in the background around 1970. (Homer Pountious collection, FMM.)

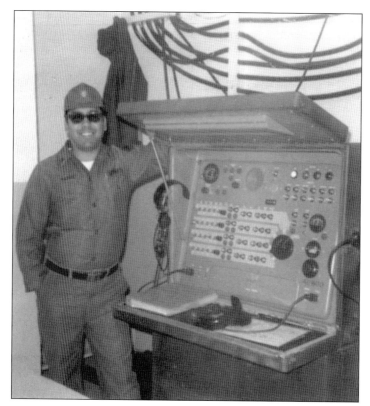

The Nike Hercules could also be controlled from inside the missile magazines. A special room adjacent to the missile storage area housed the equipment. In 1969, Ernie Alegre of D Battery is inside the launch control station at the White Point launch site (LA-43). (Ernie Alegre collection, FMM.)

In 1971, Paul Acosta and Brutus provide security for B Battery, 4th Battalion, 65th Artillery at the Malibu site (LA-78). In 1974, the Nike missile defense systems in the U.S. were closed down. It was determined by the army that the guard dogs that had been trained to kill were no longer needed. However, they were deemed too dangerous for any other uses and were euthanized. Many former crewmen relate that they feared the dogs more than the caustic fuel of the Ajax or the warheads of the Hercules. There is a cemetery on the FMM grounds where some of the Nike canines are buried. (Paul Acosta collection, FMM.)

Following the Nike era, Fort MacArthur changed dramatically. The Lower Reservation has been excavated and converted into a civilian boat harbor. The Middle Reservation (seen here around 1999) is a facility of the U.S. Air Force, while the Upper Reservation and White Point have been parceled out to the Los Angeles City Department of Recreation and Parks, Los Angeles Unified Schools, federal agencies, and non-profit groups. (FMM.)

This is Battery Osgood-Farley as it looks today, the centerpiece of the 20-acre National Historic Register Site. Housed within the battery, the Fort MacArthur Museum exhibits photographs, drawings, and artifacts from the fort's history. Long-term goals include construction of a proper museum and restoration of Battery Osgood-Farley as a historic time capsule with operational equipment. (FMM: 2003.)

ACKNOWLEDGMENTS

The authors must express sincere appreciation to numerous Fort MacArthur veterans who have helped to build the Fort MacArthur Museum's collection of photographs and artifacts into one of the finest compilations in Southern California. Over the past seven years, the collection has grown to include several thousand images, many provided by those who actually took the photograph or by members of their family. The photographs selected for this book represent some of the best.

The collection is also growing due to the generosity and assistance of local military collectors and dealers. Sometimes donating and other times selling, these individuals have made it their cause to secure Fort MacArthur related artifacts for the permanent collection. A few of the most significant items have come from Bob Chatt of Vintage Productions; Mike Constable; David George of Kaiser Bill's Emporium; Juan Gonzales of WWII Impressions; John Heague of Battlefield Adventures; David Kaufman of ASMIC; Vicki and Paul Milbury of Antique Arms; Gary Zimmer of the WWII Store; and Emory Vrana. We hope these proud supporters, and others not named, will consider this book as a tribute to their dedication to public awareness of local military heritage.

The continuing professional support of the Coast Defense Study Group, Inc. (CDSG) is gratefully acknowledged and sincerely appreciated.

The museum collection, of course, could not have grown without the support and leadership of the Fort MacArthur Museum Board of Directors. We must recognize the foresight and courage of Don Young, cofounder and first museum director, and Sam Stokes, cofounder and long-serving board officer.

We must also salute the late Col. David Gustafson, California Army National Guard, who was stationed here in the 1970s. He recognized the historic value of the site, documented it, promoted it, and helped preserve it for future generations of citizens and soldiers. His efforts laid the groundwork from which our association and museum grew.

Board members Bill Allen, Mark Berhow, Dennis DuVall, Frank Evans, Joe Janesic, Pat Murman, Rian Robison, John Palmer, and Tom Thomas were all instrumental in keeping the museum in operation through very difficult transitions.

The museum visitor's experience is shaped by our knowledgeable staff, dedicated volunteers, and generous donors, including Associated Foundations, Inc., Ted Behr, Jack Croul, Barry H. Herlihy, Marie C. Herlihy, Van and Matti Hicks, Bill and Marion Hodges, Matt and Dorothy Matich, Ralph Medina, Jean Nelson, Tom and Vivian Nelson, the Vandenbroeke family, the Vreeland family, the Demmitt family, and the Lacy family.

While the vast majority of the collection is owned and exhibited by the Fort MacArthur Museum Association, by far the largest artifact seen by the public is Battery Osgood-Farley, which houses the interpretive exhibits and is owned and operated by the City of Los Angeles Department of Recreation and Parks, led by General Manager Jon Kirk Mukri. All grounds maintenance at the museum is performed by the recreation and park staff. Through this cooperative effort, the residents of the City of Los Angeles receive the benefits of a historic asset, while the public at-large can learn about Fort MacArthur's distinguished role in the defense of our nation.